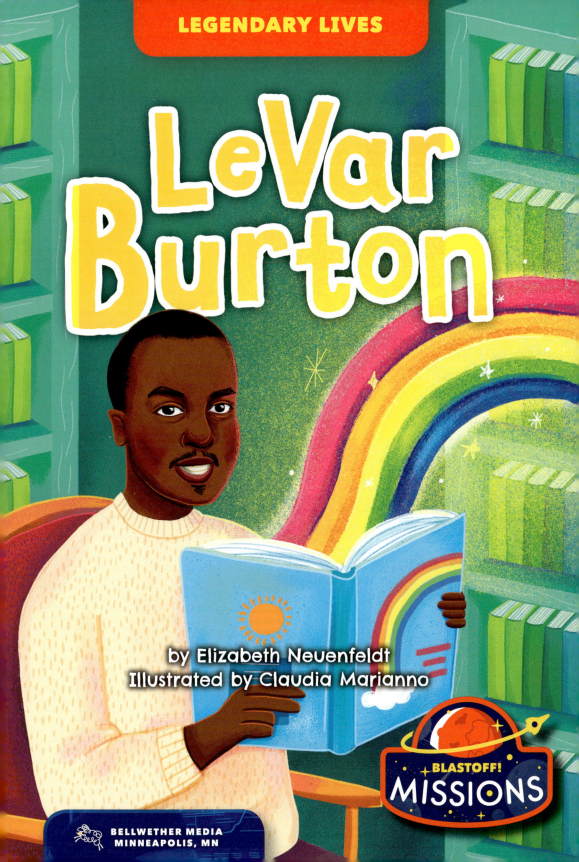

Blastoff! Missions takes you on a learning adventure! Colorful illustrations and exciting narratives highlight cool facts about our world and beyond. Read the mission goals and follow the narrative to gain knowledge, build reading skills, and have fun!

Traditional Nonfiction

Narrative Nonfiction

Blastoff! Universe

MISSION GOALS

> FIND YOUR SIGHT WORDS IN THE BOOK.

> LEARN ABOUT LEVAR BURTON'S LIFE.

> LEARN WHY READING IS IMPORTANT TO LEVAR BURTON.

This edition first published in 2026 by Bellwether Media, Inc.

No part of this publication may be reproduced in whole or in part without written permission of the publisher. For information regarding permission, write to Bellwether Media, Inc., Attention: Permissions Department, 3500 American Blvd W, Suite 150, Bloomington, MN 55431.

Library of Congress Cataloging-in-Publication Data

LC record for LeVar Burton available at: https://lccn.loc.gov/2025018593

Text copyright © 2026 by Bellwether Media, Inc. BLASTOFF! MISSIONS and associated logos are trademarks and/or registered trademarks of Bellwether Media, Inc. Bellwether Media is a division of FlutterBee Education Group.

Editor: Rebecca Sabelko   Designer: Andrea Schneider

Printed in the United States of America, North Mankato, MN.

This is **Blastoff Jimmy**! He is here to help you on your mission and share fun facts along the way!

Table of Contents

Meet LeVar Burton	4
Getting His Start	6
A Top Storyteller	12
The Next Chapter	18
Glossary	22
To Learn More	23
Beyond the Mission	24
Index	24

Meet LeVar Burton

LeVar Burton is the **host** of *Reading Rainbow*. He reads a book. Then he takes viewers on a field trip!

They read books a lot. She teaches LeVar the importance of reading.

LeVar is 17 and studying to be a **priest**. But he wants to explore more of the world.

He decides to study theater at the **University** of Southern California.

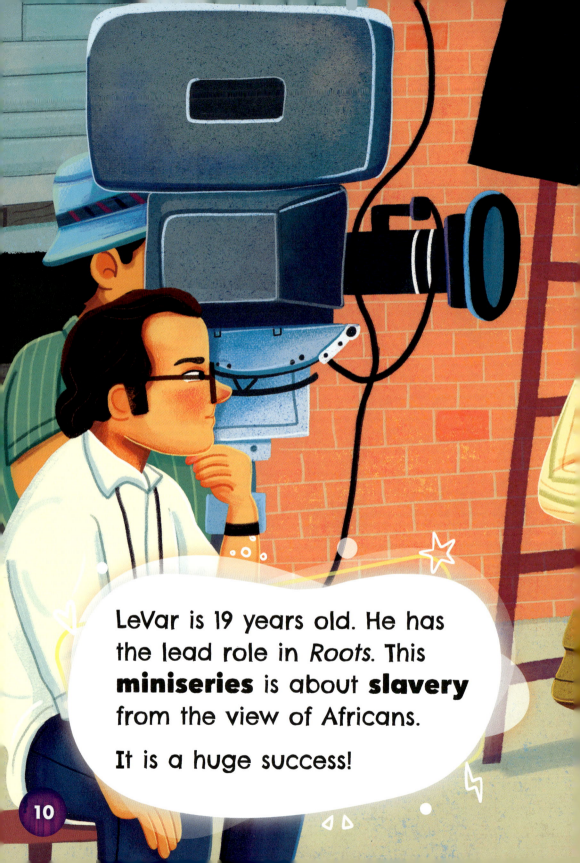

LeVar is 19 years old. He has the lead role in *Roots*. This **miniseries** is about **slavery** from the view of Africans.

It is a huge success!

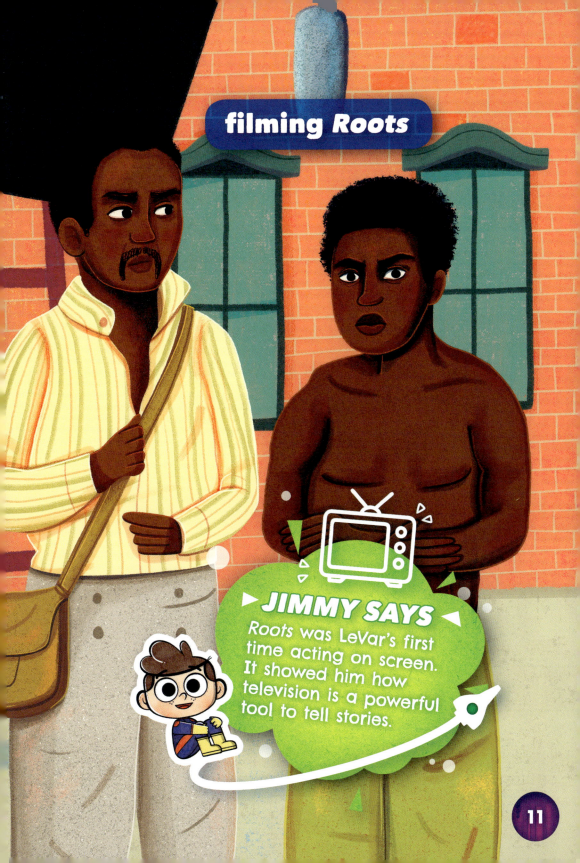

A Top Storyteller

It is now 1983. LeVar is the **producer** and host of the television show *Reading Rainbow*.

LeVar shares **diverse** books. The show teaches important lessons about the world.

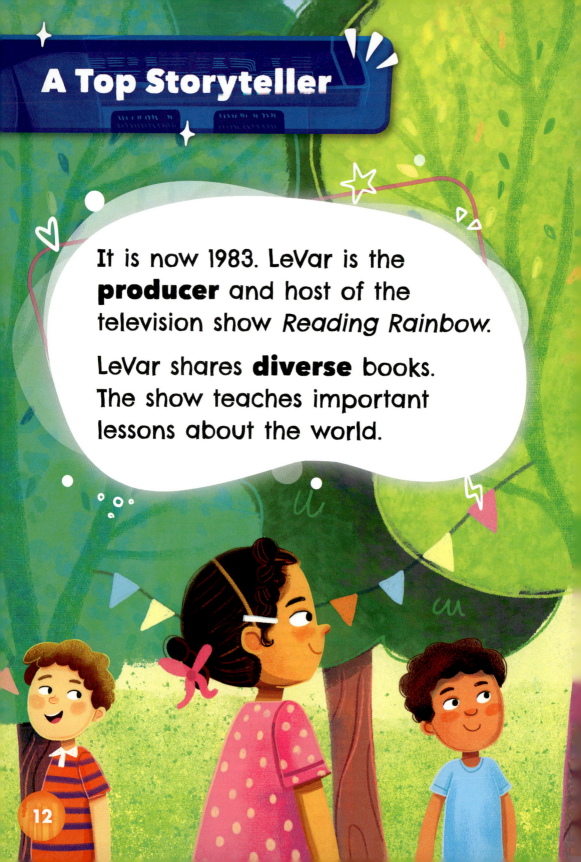

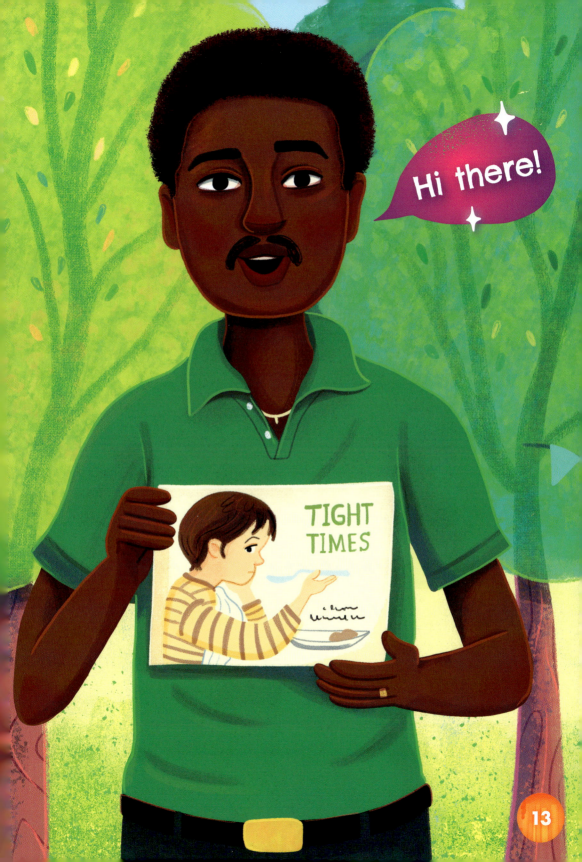

It is 1987. LeVar stars in
Star Trek: The Next Generation.

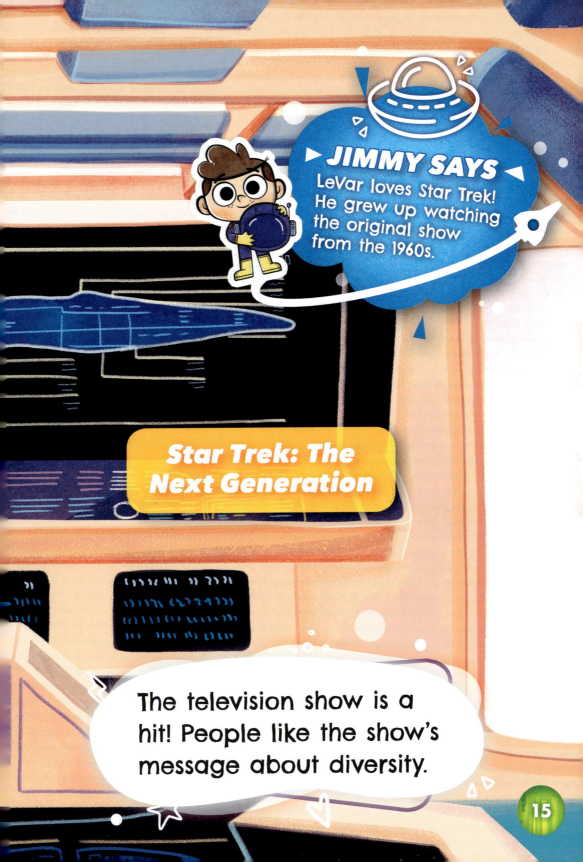

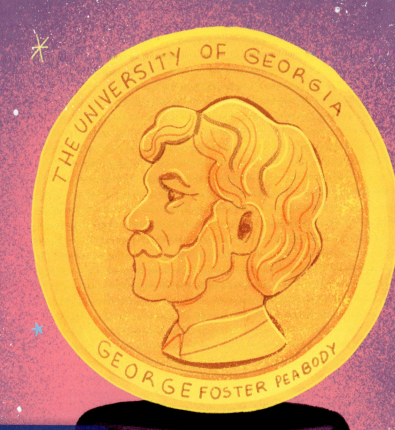

It is 1992. LeVar wins a **Peabody Award** for his work on *Reading Rainbow*.

The show ends in 2006. Thousands of children learned to love reading!

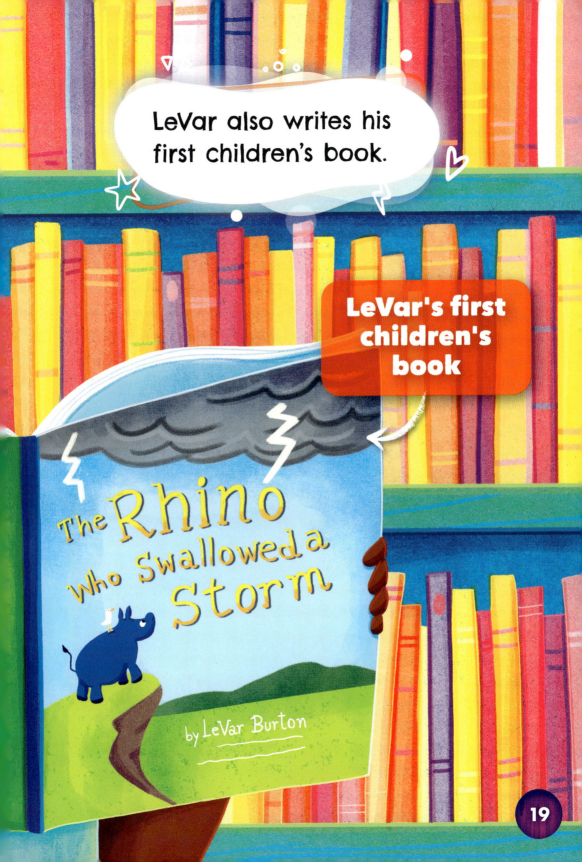

National Humanities Medal

It is 2023. LeVar produces a show about why reading is important.

Today, LeVar wins the **National Humanities Medal**. He continues to **advocate** for reading!

LeVar Burton Profile

Born
February 16, 1957, in Landstuhl, Germany

Accomplishments
Reading advocate and award-winning host and producer of Reading Rainbow, one of the longest-running children's television shows

Timeline

1977: LeVar stars in Roots

1983 to 2006: LeVar hosts and produces Reading Rainbow

1987 to 1994: LeVar is on Star Trek: The Next Generation

2012: LeVar makes an app that is now called Skybrary

2014: LeVar writes his first children's book

2023: LeVar wins the National Humanities Award

Glossary

advocate–to support and argue for a cause

app–a program such as a game or internet browser; apps are also called applications.

diverse–made up of people whose backgrounds or identities are different from one another

host–a person who talks to guests and viewers on radio or television

miniseries–a television program presented over many episodes

National Humanities Medal–an American award given each year to honor a person or group that has helped people better understand history, books, and languages

Peabody Award–an award given each year to honor a person or group that has made a positive change through storytelling

priest–a person who leads religious services

producer–a person who takes charge and provides the money to make something

slavery–the practice of owning people who work for no money

university–a school that people go to after high school

To Learn More

AT THE LIBRARY

Burton, LeVar. *A Kids Book About Imagination.* New York, N.Y.: DK Publishing, 2023.

Burton, LeVar, and Susan Schaefer Bernardo. *The Rhino Who Swallowed a Storm.* Encino, Calif.: Reading Rainbow, 2014.

Edmond, Ezra. *My Friend LeVar.* Watertown, Mass.: Charlesbridge, 2024.

ON THE WEB

FACTSURFER

Factsurfer.com gives you a safe, fun way to find more information.

1. Go to www.factsurfer.com.

2. Enter "LeVar Burton" into the search box and click 🔍.

3. Select your book cover to see a list of related content.

BEYOND THE MISSION

> WHAT FACT FROM THE BOOK DO YOU THINK WAS THE MOST INTERESTING?

> WHO DO YOU LOOK UP TO? WHY?

> WHAT IS YOUR FAVORITE BOOK? WHY DO YOU LIKE IT?

Index

app, 18
book, 4, 6, 7, 12, 18, 19
diverse, 12, 15
host, 4, 12
mom 6, 7
National Humanities Medal, 20
Peabody Award, 16, 17
priest, 9
producer, 12, 20
profile, 21
read, 4, 5, 6, 7, 17, 18, 20
Reading Rainbow, 4, 12, 17
Roots, 10, 11
slavery, 10
Star Trek: The Next Generation, 14, 15
theater, 9
University of Southern California, 9
writes, 19